NO LONGER
THE PROPERTY OF
RTDL

EXPLORE MICHIGAN

LEELANAU

Redford Township District Library
25320 West Six Mile Road
Redford, MI 48240

www.redford.lib.mi.us

Hours:

Mon-Thur 10-8:30
Fri-Sat   10-5
Sunday (School Year) 12-5

39009000339727

George Cantor has been a journalist in the Detroit area for more than 40 years. He worked for the *Detroit Free Press* and the *Detroit News* as a baseball writer, travel writer, reporter and columnist.

His proudest achievements were covering the 1968 Detroit Tigers in their championship season, raising two beautiful daughters and seeing columns he had written years ago still hanging on refrigerator doors around the state.

He also has written 15 books on sports, travel and history.

George and his wife Sherry are residents of West Bloomfield, along with their irascible west highland terrier, Charlie.

EXPLORE MICHIGAN

LEELANAU

An Insider's Guide to Michigan

George Cantor

The University of Michigan Press
Ann Arbor
&
Petoskey Publishing Company
Traverse City

RECEIVED DEC 1 6 2005

Copyright © by George Cantor, 2005
All rights reserved
Published in the United States of America by
The University of Michigan Press
Manufactured in the United States of America
Printed on acid-free paper

2008   2007   2006   2005   4   3   2   1

ISBN 0-472-03089-2

No part of this publication may be reproduced, stored in a retrieval system, or transmitted in any form or by any means, electronic, mechanical,
or otherwise, without the written permission of the publishers.

39009000339727

Library of Congress Cataloging-in-publication Data on File

Explore Michigan: Leelanau
was reviewed by Andrew
McFarland
www.absolutemichigan.com
www.leelanau.com
Cover photograph provided by
Marge Beaver, Photography Plus
www.photography-plus.com

Inside photography courtesy of
John L. Russell,
Great Lakes Images, LLC

CONTENTS

Explore Michigan: An Insider's Guide to Michigan is not meant to be a complete listing of every restaurant or every shop; it is truly meant to be an "insider's" guide. It recommends the places that the locals, and in the case of the tourist areas, long-time summer residents, know about, frequent and recommend to their family and friends.

For example, in Traverse City, the parking meters have a button that you can hit for thirty free minutes. In Leelanau County, the National Park Service conducts winter snowshoe tours of the park. In Detroit, there are cozy restaurants that out-of-towners rarely find. And if you want a more affordable, and quiet weekend at the Grand Hotel on Mackinac Island, it is now open in early spring.

Author George Cantor has been writing travel books for over twenty years. A life-long Michigander, he has traveled and explored Michigan with the gusto it takes to make these books special. Though they are guidebooks, they make for a good read before, during and after you plan to visit. George also wanted to make sure that he really had the local flare for each book in this series, so he agreed to have locals review each book and give their comments to him.

The result is *Explore Michigan: An Insider's Guide to Michigan,* where the aerial photographs on the covers by exceptionally talented Marge Beaver invite you in. Once you start reading, you are on your way to invaluable information that puts you on the inside of what our great state has to offer.

--the publishers

LEELANAU

The Top Ten Don't Miss List

1. Climb Sleeping Bear Dune.
2. If that's too strenuous, take the Pierce Stocking scenic drive to the top.
3. Stroll through the shops of Fishtown in Leland.
4. Visit one of the peninsula's outstanding wineries.
5. Take the boat trip to the Manitou islands.
6. Soak in the charm of Suttons Bay.
7. Drive M-22 along the West Arm of Grand Traverse Bay.
8. Visit the Grand Traverse Lighthouse in Northport.
9. Hike out to Pyramid Point.
10. Take a bike trip around Glen Lake.

THE TURF

A popular song of the 1940s advised: "If you can't say Acapulco, then you can call it Paradise." The same goes for the Leelanau. Hard to spell, easy to love. In the minds of many travelers, this is the paradigm of the Great Lakes experience.

Towering dunes rise sheerly from Lake Michigan. Hills rim the inland lakes. Narrow roads lead to unexpected places. There are country inns, fine restaurants and wineries. The artifacts of large scale tourism are kept at a discreet distance.

To some, it is reminiscent of California's Napa Valley. To others, the Burgundy region of France.

But the Leelanau is unique unto itself, a place that seems to defy time and change. Jarring notes are almost nonexistent, and national franchisers do not come here. There are two big reasons for that:

You don't pass through the Leelanau to get somewhere else. You come here because this is where you're going. Not a mile of federal highway runs within its boundaries.

The chains aren't especially wanted.

Some overly cute descriptions refer to the Leelanau as Michigan's "Little Finger." A glance at the Lower Peninsula map shows you why. Well, it is better, one would think, than being called the index finger, but applying the diminutive to this place is not completely inappropriate.

To use the terminology of baseball, the Leelanau is small ball. It does not overwhelm as much as it charms. It has barely 2,000 fulltime residents. Aside from its one bona fide four-star attraction, Sleeping Bear National Lakeshore, its pleasures are subtle and intimate.

No Europeans settled here until the late 1840s. Before that, the Leelanau was the home of the Ojibwa and Odawa, who sustained themselves by fishing, hunting, trading and raising a few crops. Then in the space of a few years several white communities were started. John LaRue saw an opportunity for trade with Native Americans and established a

Carp River Dam in Leland

store on Sleeping Bear Bay in 1848. It grew into the town of Glen Arbor.

In the following year, Rev. George Smith and Chief Waukazoo moved their families and a small Indian mission from the Black River area near Holland to what is now Northport, because it was the last land where Odawa could establish a permanent home.

By 1852, Rev. Peter Dougherty had decided to abandon his new cherry plantings on the Old Mission Peninsula and move his church across Grand Traverse Bay to the Leelanau for the same reason. That settlement became Omena.

During the next year, Antoine Manseau, originally from Manistee, came from North Manitou Island to build a dam at the mouth of the Carp River and open a sawmill. The dam is still a prominent feature of life in Leland.

Pioneer narratives of those years tell of a hard and iso-lated life on this distant shore. Food shortages were common. The supply line was precarious; it depended on schooners whose arrival was unpredictable. They could be delayed in rough weather or, in many cases, wrecked before they could unload their goods.

One of these calamities, the wreck of the sidewheeler *Empire* in 1849, even gave a name to the village on the adjacent shore. By 1860, however, most of these towns had docks and wooding stations. Larger ships called regularly and life grew easier.

The Leelanau followed a familiar pattern in Northern Michigan development. A small fishing-based economy was replaced by the lumbering boom in the years after the Civil War.

As navigation became easier, passenger vessels also visited these ports. The passengers liked what they saw, and by 1884 the first resort hotel was opened at Omena, in the former mission school. Just one small branch of the Grand Rapids and Indiana Railroad entered the peninsula, and that kept tourism to a trickle.

When the lumber was played out, farmers found the comparatively mild lakefront climate, and the protective snow cover of winter, ideal for fruit cultivation. This evolved into an important wine-producing industry by the late 20th Century.

The most far-reaching development, however, was establishment of the Sleeping Bear National Lakeshore in 1970. It was a highly controversial plan. Many longtime residents called it an unwarranted federal intrusion. Property owners resented having to sign finite leases on land they had owned for decades. They fought it for years before giving up.

The Lakeshore opened the Leelanau to a national market. But the much-feared tourist hordes, bringing with them a demand for bigger and better motels and burger stands, never materialized. Instead, these visitors came for the same qualities that have defined the Leelanau for generations.

A refuge from chain stores, franchised food, four-lane roads that lead to more of the same and the rush that hurried them out of the place they had just left. They come here to slow down, be surprised, and reclaim a piece of a calmer life.

And if you can't say Leelanau, then you can call it Paradise.

THE TOWNS

Leland. Although it lost the county seat to Lake Leelanau in an election in August, 2004, it is still a major destination and major shopping area. Main Street (M-22) is lined with shops for a block or two, and the old Lake Michigan dock area has been renovated as Fishtown. Here, stores are housed in weathered shacks and a market sells fish right off the boats. This is also the point of departure for ferry service to the Manitou islands.

Suttons Bay. Now the largest community in Leelanau, it sits on the eastern shore of the peninsula, in the midst of a rich fruit and vineyard area. The town is tucked into a little inlet on the West Arm of Grand Traverse Bay. It has the largest marina on the Leelanau, some interesting galleries and antique shops on St. Joseph Street. And like Leland, is very walkable, though you do have to be careful of the traffic on M-22 which cuts through the town.

Glen Arbor. Named by one of the early settlers for the profusion of wild grapes and its proximity to Glen Lake. M-22 makes a 90 degree turn here and the little downtown is clustered around that corner. Though no longer a village, as it is part of the National Lakeshore, nearly Glen Haven was the site of a Coast Guard rescue station for 43 years, coming to the aid of seamen who ran afoul of the crowded, dangerous passage between the mainland and Manitou islands.

Northport. The name describes it. The port at the tip of the Leelanau, and the busiest one during the age of sail. It was an improvement on the original name, Waukazooville, named with the best of intentions for an Odawa chief who was part of the first settling party. It is now the gateway to the lovely state park at the Leelanau's northern end.

Empire. Its Lake Michigan harbor used to be the shipping point for cut hardwood by the huge Empire Lumber Company. The company left when the mill burned down in 1917. Now the town is headquarters for Sleeping Bear National Lakeshore, with stunning views of the dunes and the islands.

Manitou Islands. Important elements in the Sleeping Bear legend (see Local Color) and about a 90-minute boat trip from the mainland. Both North and South Manitou are part of the National Lakeshore. South Manitou once had a resident community, and there are remnants of old houses, a church and a cemetery. North Manitou is maintained as wilderness.

LOCAL COLOR

Sleeping Bear and D.H. Day

Maybe it was the legend, a tale right out of *Aesop's Fables.* The eastern shoreline of Lake Michigan is lined with dunes, after all; all the way from the Indiana Border to the mouth of Grand Traverse Bay.

The French explorers of the coast barely made mention of this 460-foot high mountain of sand. It was just one of many. So why should this particular dune become the centerpiece of a National Lakeshore? Because as 19th Century folklorists began assembling Native American stories, they heard the tale of the Sleeping Bear and her cubs. And it has become one of the best-loved legends in Michigan.

The Ojibwa told of a mother bear and her two cubs fleeing a massive forest fire on the Wisconsin side of the lake. She plunged into the water and urged her babies to follow. After swimming many miles, she finally reached the Michigan shore and lay down to await the arrival of her cubs. But they grew tired, and before they could join their mother they drowned.

Empire beach

The Great Spirit took pity on the bears. The mother went to sleep for eternity and formed the giant dune. The cubs became North and South Manitou islands.

The story has a timeless, irresistible appeal. One of the first to realize that was a lumberman, David H. Day. His company was based in Glen Arbor and it made him rich. He became a major landowner in the Leelanau. But he looked ahead to the day when the stands of hardwood were played out. On what would the local economy be based then? One answer was fruit-growing, and Day turned 5,000 acres of his land into orchard. He also understood, though, that the natural beauty of the area held even greater potential.

He began running steamships between Glen Arbor and the cities of Chicago and Milwaukee to carry vacationers here in the 1880s. He promoted the great dune at his doorstep by building a resort hotel, which he named the Sleeping Bear Inn.

When the automobile arrived, Day was among the first to grasp that this changed everything. He organized the West Michigan Resort Association and became an ardent supporter of the Good Roads Movement, calling for a national network of paved highways. One result of his work was the construction of M-22, the road that follows the Leelanau shore all the way around the peninsula.

Day also was named the first chairman of Michigan's State Park Commission. In 1919, he decided to set an example by donating 32 acres of his own lakefront property to the State. This was the first public land in the Sleeping Bear area and laid the foundation for the National Lakeshore, which now surrounds it.

Day died in 1929, but his family remained active in promoting tourism in the area for decades. The D.H. Day Farm with its picturesque barns, are a must shoot for photographers.

William Beals and the Leelanau School

A generation of boys called him "Skipper." Beals and his wife, Cora Mautz Beals, were co-founders of Glen Arbor's Leelanau School, recognized today as a fine prep school that has remained true to its origins.

The Beals were young faculty members of the Principia, a Christian Science academy in St. Louis, Mo., when they came here on vacation in 1921. They fell in love with property at the mouth of the Crystal River and decided it would be the perfect spot for their dream; a summer educational camp that also would instruct boys on self-reliance.

Two years later, Camp Leelanau was a reality. The campers lived, at first, in tents right on the beach, and a close relationship with the natural world was encouraged. Several of the campers and their families urged the Beals to expand the camp into a year-round facility. So in 1929 it became the Leelanau School, with 15 young men enrolled in grades 9 and 10.

Over the years, the prep school became co-educational and, despite the wan economy of the 30s, it expanded into a full secondary institution. It always has emphasized environmental studies as a core of the curriculum, as well as writing.

The year the school opened, the Beals completed construction of a permanent classroom and dormitory building and their own permanent residence. They called their house the Homestead. Through a succession of land exchanges, this became the basis of the Homestead Resort, ranked as one of the finest in Michigan. The school and resort occupy adjacent parcels of land, although the entrances are separate.

William Beals died in 1942, but the school remained under family ownership, run by a former camper who married Cora's sister. Cora Mautz Beals remained actively engaged with the Board of Trustees until her own death in 1996.

WHERE TO STAY

Top of the Line

The Homestead Resort. North of Glen Arbor, off M-22. (231) 334-5100.

On a splendid Lake Michigan beach, with the Crystal River running through it, and a ski hill in the surrounding forest, this is one of the State's standout vacation properties. There are a variety of accommodations: An inn that was originally built as the Leelanau School dorm, a couple of smaller lodges scattered around the property, and private condominiums that rent out by the day or week. Rates run from under $100 for a basic unit back in the woods, to $500 for a family condo on the water. There are several swimming pools, a spa, tennis courts, a 9-hole golf course, and float equipment. What tops it off is the minimally invasive footprint it leaves on the environment. This is a first class operation all the way.

Other Choices

Falling Waters Lodge. Main Street, Leland. (231) 256-9832.

If location counts for anything, this place is aces. It is in the midst of downtown Leland, just steps from Fishtown, right on the millrace leading to the lake. The Lodge boasts that you can walk onto a balcony from a first floor room and fish from there. No pool. Room costs are in the mid $100s.

Leland Lodge. 565 Pearl Street, Leland.
(231) 256-9848.

Just a few blocks east of Main Street, and an easy walk to downtown. Adjacent to the golf course of the Leland Country Club. Pleasant and cozy accommodations in 18 rooms. Top rooms face the course and go for about $200 a night; others are in the low $100s range. No pool.

Bed and Breakfast

This is the more typical kind of Leelanau accommodation; small scale with a touch of history thrown in. Here is a sampling.

Sleeping Bear Bed and Breakfast. 11977 S. Gilbert Road, Empire. (231) 326-5375.

A farmhouse built around 1889, just off M-72, a few miles east of Empire and a few miles south of Glen Lake. A quiet getaway in a hilly setting, just minutes from most of the attractions of the Sleeping Bear Lakeshore. Five bedrooms, lovely gardens, specialty French toast for breakfast. Susan and Van Wilson are the hosts.

Whaleback Inn. 1757 N. Manitou Trail (M-22), one mile south of Leland. (231) 256-9090.

On a hill overlooking Lake Leelanau, five acres of grounds, with 14 rooms in a main lodge and cottages. There is a sundeck, walking trails, children's play area. Most rooms have views of the lake. This is a good choice for families.

Glen Arbor Bed and Breakfast. 6548 Western Avenue (M-22), Glen Arbor. (231) 334-6789.

Right in the middle of this lakeside village, this 1880s farmhouse has been redone in French country style, with a white-pillared front porch and gardens in the front. Just steps from Lake Michigan beaches, downtown stores and restaurants. There are six rooms and suites, two of them sharing a bath. Try the Good Harbor Suite, with a private deck, queen bed and sleeper. There are also two free-standing cottages on the grounds.

Korner Kottage Bed and Breakfast. 503 N. St. Joseph Avenue, Suttons Bay. (231) 271-2711.

A block north of the business district, on M-22, with views of the marina and bay. This is a Craftsman style home, built in the 1920s. It has three rooms, two upstairs and one on the main floor, all with private bath. Innkeeper Sharon Sutterfield doesn't believe in naming her rooms, but try the upstairs king at $155 a night. Spacious and bright.

Omena Sunset Lodge. 12819 Tatch Road (County 626), Omena. (231) 386-9080.

The main house dates from 1898 and is situated on a ridge overlooking Grand Traverse Bay, just west of this historic village. There are 12 rooms in the main house and two cottages on the grounds. Guests in the more remote Dixie LeMieux Cottage have the option of getting breakfast brought to their door. Rates run between $90 and $140.

Days Gone By. 201 N. High Street, Northport. (231) 386-5114.

The place is well-named. The house itself dates from 1868, decor of the five rooms is mostly Victorian and the stonework is evocative of earlier times--from the four-foot wall that encircles the house to the outdoor fireplace. The Native American room is very popular, with furnishings inspired by local Indian lore. It also has a great clawfoot tub. Complimentary local wines are served in the evening. On a residential street, just a few blocks from downtown.

A Winery Choice

Inn at Black Star Farms. 10844 E. Revold Road, Suttons Bay. (231) 271-4970.

This may be the most beautifully situated of any of Leelanau's 11 wineries. The eight-room inn is surrounded by hillsides terraced in vineyards. Walking and riding trails lead off into the countryside. There is a working dairy farm on the property, as well as tasting rooms. It is as close to the Napa Valley vineyards as you will find in Leelanau. It is located south of Suttons Bay, on a narrow road that runs between M-22 and County 633.

Camping

There is one campground in the Leelanau portion of Sleeping Bear National Lakeshore and several more on the Manitou islands.

D.H. Day is open from April through November, with 88 sites available on a first-come, first-served basis. The location is excellent, near the town of Glen Haven and just up the road (M-109) from the Dune Climb and Lake Michigan beaches. A park pass is necessary to get in, a $12 fee per night is charged and there is a 14-night maximum.

There is water, vault toilets and nightly campfire programs led by a park ranger during the summer.

On **South Manitou**, camping is permitted at three locations with a total of 51 sites on a first come basis. There is no motorized transportation to any of them, and everything must be carried in. Bay and Weather Station Campgrounds are within a reasonable walk of the boat landing, but Popple, with its 6 sites, is at the farthest end of the island and recommended only for those who seek solitude.

North Manitou is 15,000 acres of wilderness and you are free to pitch a tent wherever you find a likely spot.

Manitou Island Transit (231-256-9061), running out of Leland, provides daily transportation to both islands. A permit must be obtained for camping on both islands and can be purchased at the boat dock. The daily camping fee is $5. Cost of the ferry trip is $25 for adults and $14 for 12 and under.

Leelanau State Park has 52 rustic sites (water and vault toilets) on the Lake Michigan shore. Call (800) 447-2757 for reservations. The park entrance is off County Road 629, north of Northport.

Lake Leelanau RV Park is situated on 700 feet of shoreline, with a private beach and boat rentals available. There are 196 sites, structured for big vehicles. It is located at 3101 Lake Shore Drive (County Road 643), south of Leland. (231) 256-7236.

Sleepy Bear Campground caters to both hook-ups and tent campers. There is a swimming pool, playground, store and modern restrooms on its wooded 70-acres with 190 sites. It is located off M-72 (Empire Highway), six miles east of Empire. (231) 326-5566.

Wild Cherry Resort is geared to RVers. It sits on a lake, and 25 of its 50 sites are situated upon the water. Lots of modern amenities and even a golf course that is nearing completion. It is located on 8563 E. Horn Road, which runs north from M-204, halfway between Suttons Bay and Lake Leelanau. (231) 271-5550.

Condo and Cottage Rentals

Leelanau Vacation Rentals is the largest agency of its kind on the peninsula. From its base in Glen Harbor it handles 120 properties, including condos at the Homestead. Some of the private homes on its list are expansive residences on prime Glen Lake locations. (231) 334-6100.

Nature's Rentals has eleven properties to choose from in Leelanau County (877-228-8558 or 231-275-4500). They reach from Little Glen to Leland, with quite a few on tranquil Little Traverse Lake.

EATING OUT

La Becasse. Burdickville. (231) 334-3944.

Serious critics rate this one of the finest tables in the entire State. It is contemporary French cuisine and the menu changes annually based on the research of its owners. Reservations are required in this intimate setting. It's near the southeastern corner of Glen Lake, at the corner of County Roads 616 and 675. A bit out of the way, but worth every mile of the journey.

Maple Leaf Restaurant. Maple City. (231) 228-4688.

The building dates from 1866 when it was a wooden peg factory. It later became the town schoolhouse, and that's the ambience its owners have retained. Despite the name, you're not going to find Canadian specialties here. That's a relief, eh? Quite the opposite, in fact, in that the chef likes to bring in a lot of Southwest overtones to the regional dishes on the menu. Its Sunday brunch is superb. It's at 172 W. Burdickville Road (County Road 616).

North—A Centennial Inn. (231) 386-5087.

Northport resident, Nick Vandenbelt, along with the former chef of La Becasse, have purchased the Leelanau Country Inn and renamed it North—A Centennial Inn. It's on M-22, about midway between Leland and Glen Arbor.

Funistrada. (231) 334-3900.

Formerly the Glen Lake Inn, the outside doesn't look too special, but don't let that fool you. They have excellent Italian fare with a superb atmosphere. Open six days a week in the summer and more limited in the off-season, so call ahead. Not too far from LaBecasse, as it is just south of where County Roads 616 and 675 meet.

The **Bluebird.** Leland. (231) 256-9081.

Legendary is not a word to toss around lightly, but this landmark in downtown Leland probably has a greater claim to it than any other dining establishment in the area. It has been serving up its celebrated whitefish since 1927. The Bluebird is right across the street from the Fishtown docks and it doesn't get much fresher than that. It is also renowned for its cinnamon rolls, which may not be the best accompaniment to the local wines it serves but are delectable nonetheless. At 102 E. River Street.

Café Bliss. Suttons Bay. (231) 271-5000.

With a name like this you'd better be good. The bliss builds from a vegetarian base, but has expanded to include a fully rounded menu. The set-up is reminiscent of a Victorian tea room, but don't let that put you off. It is quite a romantic little place and the desserts are classic. There is garden dining in warm weather. On the main street, at 420 St. Joseph Avenue.

Hattie's. 111 St. Joseph Street, Sutton's Bay. 231 271-6222.

The restaurant was sold in 2004 to the former executive chef at Boyne Highlands. During its previous 18 years, Hattie's had won an outstanding reputation for its blend of Asian and California-style food with Michigan ingredients, such as morel mushroom ravioli. In a storefront in downtown Sutton's Bay, with minimalist décor.

Key to the County. Lake Leelanau. (231) 256-5397.

An apt name for a place that sits near the geographic heart of the Leelanau. It's right on Main Street, M-204, near the bridge across the Lake Leelanau narrows. It also measures up well to the other choices in the area, with its menu of fresh seafood (the crabcakes are exceptional) and locally grown produce. The ambience is nice, too, in a century old saloon that has been upgraded.

The **Riverside Inn.** Leland. (231) 256-9971.

As the name indicates, this place sits right beside the Leland River, a few blocks east of the business district, at 302 E. River Street. The menu changes with the season, usually featuring lake fish, game and local fruit, with hints of Asian fusion. A deck overlooking the water invites outdoor dining in summer. The place has been here since 1905, so it's shown some staying power.

Casual Meals

Joe's Friendly Tavern. 11015 Front Street, Empire.

What the Bluebird is to whitefish, Joe's is to burgers. Always near the head of the lists of top bar food in the State and the town's top gathering place. And, true to its promise, it is friendly.

Canoes Up North Grill and Lucky Duck Tavern. 201 St. Joseph, Suttons Bay.

The name alone would make it. But this comfortable place, built around a two-story stone fireplace, gets on the list with its Italian and Mexican specialties and robust breakfasts. The Lucky Duck also claims to be the oldest eating place in the Leelanau.

Western Avenue Grill. On M-22, in Glen Arbor.

Lively bar, terrific whitefish, an extensive menu and an Up North setting that even extends to canoes hanging from the ceiling.

Steak-Haus at King's Challenge. South from M-22, between Glen Arbor and Leland.

On the 18th green of the Homestead's golf course, locals call this the best steak house in the Leelanau. Of course, it is also the only steak house in the Leelanau, but it lives up to that responsibility, not only with terrific beef, but stellar pork chops and lamb dishes, too.

Sugarfoot Saloon. North of Cedar on County Road 651 at Bodus Road.

Best ribs in the area, good walleye, some Mexican entrees, and you will hate yourself if you don't leave room for the homemade pies.

Eat Spot. 25 Mill Street, Northport.

The name doesn't get more basic than this, but the place is a little charmer. Best bet is the salads, which are known for inventive ingredients. There is also a good sandwich menu and some pizza.

Stone House Cafe

Stone House Café. 407 S. Main, Leland.

Bob Pisor was a veteran Detroit journalist and a good one, who wised up and got into the bread-making racket. He has expanded his operation to include all the things that go between the slices of his excellent home-made bread.

Boone's Prime Time Pub. 102 St. Joseph, Suttons Bay.

Boone's is a family-owned restaurant company that runs several good eating places in the Traverse City-Leelanau area. Most of them concentrate on beef raised on its own cattle ranch. The Suttons Bay place is the oldest of the group and even has a nice fireplace in the log cabin-style room. They also own Boonedock's in Glen Arbor, a very popular place in the summer, with live entertainment on many nights. Boonedock's is also open year-round for those cold nights you are in Glen Arbor and looking for a warm meal.

Thyme Out. 6453 Western Avenue, Glen Arbor.

The best pastry shop in the area and the perfect spot for a contemplative breakfast in the garden on a wonderful summer morning. They also make up terrific picnic baskets.

The **Cove.** 111 River Street, Leland.

It gets a little fancy inside, but if you want to sit on the deck beside the millrace and look out over the Fishtown area, this is the place for a satisfying lunch.

Art's Tavern. 6487 Western Avenue, Glen Arbor.

Another in a distinguished line of local places that serve up top-drawer whitefish and burgers. Art's also offers smelt all year round, good news for those who crave the little devils.

WALKING AND SHOPPING

There are no cities in the Leelanau. This much is true. But its villages call out for exploration. Shops and galleries can be found along their main streets and in hidden away corners. Most walks lead to water vistas, too.

Glen Arbor

The town is tucked in between Sleeping Bear Bay and Glen Lake, surrounded by resorts and the National Lakeshore. Right at its center is the corner of Manitou Trail and Western Avenue, thoroughfares that are otherwise known as M-22 and M-109.

There is seldom a parking problem, so just leave your car on the street. A good place would be in front of the Village Sampler on Manitou.

This is pleasant mini-mall with an assortment of eight shops on the premises. Look into **Black Swan,** closest to the street, which has been selling resort wear and designer apparel since 1987. A bit more casual is **Dune Wear,** with its collection of tees and sweats. **Tiny Treasures** is one of the area's best toy stores and the **Yarn Shop,** at the back of the mall, features original hand-knit sweaters.

Cross Western Avenue and turn left. Halfway down the block is the **Ruth Conklin Gallery**, among the most highly regarded on the Leelanau. The owner fashions stools and clocks from local materials, and the gallery also showcases the work of Leelanau artists in driftwood carvings and furniture. Next door, in the **Lake Isle Shops,** is the jewelry studio of Susan Hepburn-Holt, and **Bittersweet,** a fine antiques store.

Across Western is another of the area's top galleries, **Synchronicity.** It features contemporary works by more than 100 Michigan artists in a variety of media.

Now head back toward Manitou on the same side of the street. Past the intersection, you'll come upon the **Totem Shop,** one of the great Up North souvenir outposts. It's been selling Indian moccasins, Petoskey stones, fudge and the other accoutrements of a Leelanau experience for more than 70 years.

Turn right at Lake Street, and there is another cluster of shops. **Cottonseed** and **Flying Colors** are worth looking into for more ideas in jewelry, home design and clothing.

At the end of this block is **Cherry Republic,** with an astonishing variety of food products made out of the star local fruit. Everything from pies to cookies to ice cream sodas. The owners claim they have 130 different food products in which cherries are the prime ingredient. You can believe it. There are also gorgeous flower gardens here.

Across the street is **Lake Street Studios,** featuring a collection of local artists working in copper, glass, wrought iron, flowers...you name it.

The **Cottage Book Shop,** in the log cabin halfway down

the block, is one of the best for regional material, and a keen selection of novels that they always seem to correctly recommend. They also have a knack for finding good books that don't always hit the mainstream markets.

You can finish off this walk by continuing one more block along Lake Street to Lake Michigan. Or, if you have worked up an appetite, you have an abundance of choices. **Art's Tavern** is right at the corner of Lake and Western, while the **Western Avenue Grill** and the baked delights of **Thyme Out** are just a few steps away.

Suttons Bay

There is no trick to finding your way around this place. St. Joseph Avenue (M-22) is the main stem and it has preserved much of its 19th Century ambience. In the two blocks between Madison and Adams streets you'll find one of the most intensive concentrations of galleries and antique stores in the North.

By actual count, there are nine of them. Among the most interesting to look for:

Michigan Artists Gallery, with an assortment of state artists in various media, featuring the fiber work of Chris Triola. They also exclusively feature Char Bickel, whose images of bears, and other animals, and people, are framed in magical shadow boxes, with mats of torn sheet music, maps and silk leaves. She is one of northern Michigan's most collected artists.

Applegate Collection, with an amplitude of antiques, and an especially fine collection of wicker products.

Up North Antiques, which specializes in material from this area.

Suttons Bay Galleries, just off this strip, on Jefferson Street, concentrates on fine art and rare antiques, and **Treeline** is on Adams Street.

Along St. Joseph is **Bahle's,** one of the oldest clothing stores in the State, doing business here since 1876.

By the Bay Scrapbooking is a unique operation that carries a full line of everything you need to start a personal album—the perfect summer project.

Lima Bean prides itself on its quirky and eclectic selection of women's clothing and accessories.

Michigan Peddler also has outlets on Mackinac Island and Mackinaw City, but this was the original. It carries only food and gifts that are made in Michigan, along with 50 different state wines.

Front Porch specializes in stuff for the kitchen.

Enerdyne, with a wonderful assortment of educational toys and games. There is also **Known Books,** which has an excellent selection of used books, bestsellers, regional titles and a superb collection of children's books—many of them autographed. They also carry autographed copies of local author and astronaut Jerry Linnenger, who it is not uncommon to see in the store browsing or shopping.

While we're on the subject of education, you may want to walk down to Dame Street, a block south of Madison, and look in at the **Inland Seas Education Association.** The *Inland Seas* is a 77-foot schooner, anchored at the end of this block.

During the school year, groups are taken aboard for cruises that introduce them to the ecology and folklore of the Great Lakes and the mysteries of sail. In summer months, family groups may also make reservations.
Call (231) 271-3077 for more information or drop by the offices here.

You can follow the wooden walkway out to the ship, then back along the south end of the city marina to St. Joseph and the start of this walk.

Leland

Some people insist this place was named because it is on the lee-ward side of the big lake. But it seems just as likely that the body of water at its back door, Lake Leelanau, attached its name to the village.

The only problem with that theory is that the lake was originally called Carp Lake, and the stream running through the middle of town was the Carp River. Since there are lots of other Michigan lakes and rivers named for that fish, the lake's name was changed to Leelanau and the river became the Leland. Which sort of leaves us right back where we started.

Even Leelanau itself is a name of suspicious origin. It was devised by Indian agent and ethnographer Henry Schoolcraft who said it was Ojibwa and meant, "Delight of life." Later language experts have caught Schoolcraft in several Indian-sounding word inventions, though, and this may very well be one of them.

Whatever the case, Leland occupies the neck of land between Lake Michigan and Lake Leelanau. Its Main Street is M-22 and it has the highest concentration of shops. Leave the car near the corner of Main and River and set off to explore from there.

Leelanau Books

There are several galleries and clothing stores here and right around the corner on Lake Street. Look especially for **Molly's,** which has an exceptionally nice assortment of fashionable sweaters, and for the **M. Frey Studio,** owned by local watercolorist Mary Frey. It faces the harbor. On Main Street is **Leelanau Books,** which carries an excellent selection of hardcover titles, regional books, nature books and guidebooks, novels, children's books. If you are in Leland and need a read—stop here. The staff is also a great help and know their material.

The most interesting part of Leland, however, is **Fishtown;** the collection of weathered grey shacks on the water. Where the Leland River tumbles down its mill run and into Lake Michigan, fishermen of the late 19th Century built sheds to unload and process the day's catch.

Commercial fishing sustained the town well into the 1920s and Carlson's Fisheries is the last of the original operations. It began in 1906 and is now run by the fifth generation of the family. Several Leelanau restaurants serve their whitefish, or you can buy it yourself right off the boats at their store here.

Even when fishing declined and most of these shacks were deserted, Carlson's kept going at the same stand. Fishtown finally was restored in the 1970s and is now on the National Register of Historic Places.

A good bet for a picnic lunch is the **Village Cheese Shanty,** another Fishtown mainstay. It caters to travelers bound for the Manitou islands, since it is located just a few steps from the ferry dock. But you can stay right on land and enjoy one of their oversized sandwiches, too.

Follow the river up from Fishtown and make a right on Main. In a block you will come to the **Old Art Building,** a center of community life since 1922.

It was originally built as a women's club and cultural center. The building was donated to Michigan State University in 1939, and for 50 years the school held summer art classes here. When they were discontinued, the community raised funds to restore the building to its original function as a cultural center. It now holds art classes and exhibits local artists throughout the year.

Walk back on Main to River Street. The landmark **Bluebird Restaurant** is located at this corner, and a few more blocks will bring you to another excellent eating place, the **Riverside Inn**. This is a more tranquil part of Leland and you can peek through white picket fences to see backyard gardens.

A right on Chandler Street will take you to the **Leelanau Historical Museum** (described in Things to See) which is worth a stop. Afterwards, keep walking along Chandler to the river's outlet to Lake Leelanau.

You can extend the walk a bit by turning east on Juniper Trail, then left on Fifth Street, past the Leland Country Club. If you can get on this quiet private course, it is worth it. Another left on Pearl Street will bring you back to the middle of town.

At the corner of Pearl and Main is the Village Green, preserved from development by local funding and the **Leelanau Conservancy.** The little park, with the huge maple at its center and cobblestone walkways leading through it, has become a community gathering place, and it's the perfect spot to relax and watch the life of the village flow past.

SLEEPING BEAR DUNES NATIONAL LAKESHORE

The glaciers retreated at the end of the last Ice Age, almost 12,000 years ago. They left behind deep basins that were filled by melting ice and rainfall to become the Great Lakes. Ridges of glacial sediment cut off inland bodies of water from Lake Michigan. As the prevailing western winds blew over the centuries, they picked up sand particles and deposited them along these ridges to form dunes. The Ojibwa legend is much better (see Local Color), but in geologic terms that's how the Sleeping Bear National Lakeshore was created.

The dunes

It was the vision of a small group of Michigan environ-
mentalists who saw it as a way to preserve an irreplaceable
part of the Great Lakes. The bill proposing it was quietly
introduced in Congress in 1959, part of a much larger package of legislation that created a series of national seashores
and lakeshores, from Cape Cod to the Oregon coast.

To many local residents, it looked very much like a federal land grab. They came out by the thousands at public
hearings to voice their displeasure and denounce its back-
ers. The battle over Sleeping Bear lasted for more than a
decade and the bitterness it aroused didn't subside for many
years afterwards, but Michigan's U.S. Senator Philip A.
Hart believed in the vision and steadfastly supported the
legislation until its final approval by Congress in 1970.

The park that exists today encompasses 35 miles of
lakeshore in Benzie and Leelanau counties, as well as North
and South Manitou islands. Besides the natural features, it
also preserves much of the area's history around the village
of Glen Haven. A general store, Coast Guard life-saving station, boathouse and blacksmith shop may be visited there.

There is a $10 entrance fee for private vehicles; $5 for
hikers and bikers.

The best way to get acquainted with the park is to stop by its visitor center in Empire. It explains the history of the area through a slide presentation, "Dreams of the Sleeping Bear," and also exhibits artifacts from dune country. The center, named after Senator Hart, is located on M-72, just east of M-22, and is open daily, 8 a.m. to 6 p.m., Memorial Day to Labor Day; 9 a.m. to 4 p.m., rest of the year.

Attractions

The most photographed part of the park is the **Dune Climb**. The image of ascending human forms dwarfed by the mountain of gleaming white sand is an unforgettable sight.

It's not quite the natural experience that the park organizers envisioned. The ambience is more like a sack race at the annual Labor Day company picnic. But that's a quibble. It's lots of fun, as family groups leave their shoes at the bottom of the dune and start climbing up through the shifting sand.

Only the hearty make it to the top, but even a partial climb rewards participants with wonderful views back to Glen Lake. Besides, it's great exercise. The parking area is right off M-109, the main roadway through the park.

Pierce Stocking Scenic Drive

This magnificent 7.5 mile road was opened in 1967, the pet project of the veteran lumberman for whom it is named. Stocking roamed the dunes as a young man and understood that their most beautiful areas were accessible only to those vigorous enough to make the steep climb through the sand. He conceived of this drive while the debate over the national lakeshore was heating up and operated it as a private toll road until his death in 1976. It was then incorporated into the Lakeshore.

For most of its length, this is a narrow, one-way loop, with lots of sharp curves. It passes through deep forest and there is even a covered bridge along the route. The overlooks above Lake Michigan are among the most spectacular viewpoints in the state and there are places to stop for picnics nearby.

The road is closed during rainy or foggy weather, opening in daylight hours from mid-April through Veterans Day. The entrance fee is part of the National Lakeshore admission. The road begins at M-109, just south of the Dune Climb.

Pierce Stocking Scenic Drive with covered bridge

Glen Haven General Store, Boathouse and Blacksmith Shop

All of these historic buildings are located in the village of Glen Haven, just off M-109 as it makes its turn toward Glen Arbor. Its location on Sleeping Bear Bay made Glen Haven one of the busiest ports in the Leelanau into the early 20th Century.

The store has been restored to its appearance of the 1920s. It carries merchandise typical of the period and items relating to the history of the dunes area. There is also a small museum.

The boathouse was once the fruit cannery of local businessman D.H. Day (see Local Color), one of the first boosters of the dunes as a tourist destination. It displays vessels used in fishing and Coast Guard life-saving operations, as well as the original Edison generator that supplied electric power to the entire town.

The nearby blacksmith shop also appears as it would have in the 1920s, with demonstrations of the many purposes for which iron was used in that era.

The buildings are open daily, July 1 to Labor Day, 11 a.m. to 4 p.m.; other hours vary but they generally open on Memorial Day weekend.

Sleeping Bear Point Maritime Museum

The **Manitou Passage,** between the mainland and South Manitou Island, was one of the most dangerous stretches of water on the Great Lakes. By official count, 58 shipwrecks went down off Glen Haven, and parts of these vessels still wash up on the beaches.

In 1902, the U.S. Coast Guard opened a rescue station here. It operated for 40 years, although it had to be moved in the 1930s when shifting sands threatened to engulf it.

The station was abandoned for 42 years, until being turned into a museum in 1984. There are exhibits on the most famous wrecks in this area, daily demonstrations of rescue techniques with the line-throwing Lyle cannon, and some original Coast Guard boats. The second floor has been turned into a reconstruction of a pilot house of a lake freighter.

The museum is open daily, 10:30 a.m. to 5 p.m., late May to Labor Day; weekends only, to mid-October.

Hiking Trails

There are 11 trails within the Leelanau County portion of the Lakeshore and each of them explores a different aspect of the dunes environment. Many of these trails pass by private land, and property rights should be respected. Going from south to north, the trails are these:

Empire Bluff. South of Empire, off Wilco Road. This is a 1.5 mile trail that leads to a 400-foot high overlook on Lake Michigan. It passes a deserted farm, a planted-over logging area and a splendid beech and maple climax forest. This is a magnificent view and in the summer, quite common to see hangliders taking off from the bluff. Bring your camera and see if you can match local photographers like Terry Phipps, Ken Scott and others, who all have captured the magic.

Windy Moraine. East from M-109, at Welch Road. This 1.5 mile loop is rated advanced for both hikers and cross-country skiers because of steep descents. Great overlooks of the dunes and Glen Lake.

Shauger Hill. Off the Pierce Stocking Drive, west of M-109. This 2.4 mile trail more or less parallels the scenic road and crosses it twice, so hikers should be aware of the presence of cars. In other places, it runs through a deeply forested area of the dune.

Cottonwood. (Summer only). It begins at roadside stop number four on Pierce Stocking Drive. This 1.5 mile walk is recommended for families, although the portion that runs through loose sand can be strenuous.

The **Dunes.** (Summer only). This is the 3.5 mile trail that begins at the Dune Climb, off M-109. It is a tough climb to the top, although once the summit is gained, the views are spectacular. Take a sun hat.

Duneside Accessible. (Summer only.) This is a trail designed for wheelchairs, the visually impaired or those who have problems walking. It runs for 2.9 miles along the base of the dunes and passes through a variety of forest environments. A tape cassette describing the walk may be purchased at park headquarters.

Sleeping Bear Point. (Summer only.) The 2.8 mile trail begins at the Coast Guard Station museum, just west of Glen Haven. It is a mildly difficult walk along the rolling dunes, with views of the lake and fields of wildflowers on the way.

Alligator Hill. There are 8.6 miles of trails in the land between the dunes and Glen Lake, ranging from easy to advanced. The grade depends on the climb involved, although all have views of the inland lake. The trailhead is south from M-109 on Stocking Road (not the scenic drive) or east from the highway on Day Forest Road.

Bay View. This 10-mile trail leads to the view at Lookout Point, leading through dense forest, abandoned farms and pine plantations. It can be picked up on the grounds of the Homestead Resort or on Thoreson Road, which branches north from M-22, north of Glen Arbor.

Pyramid Point. Many hikers say this 2.7 mile trail is the best in the lakeshore, and among the top hiking experiences in Michigan. It leads to a bluff high above the lake, but in a much more isolated area than the Dune Climb. It passes through meadows and forest on the way and it is a fairly strenuous trip. Take Port Oneida Road north from M-22, to Basch Road, and leave the car there.

Good Harbor Bay. Another good experience for families, over mostly flat terrain and some swampy areas between the dunes and Little Traverse Lake. It runs 2.8 miles. Take County Road 669 north from M-22, then turn right on Lake Michigan Road to reach the trailhead.

Manitou Islands

For those with time and a taste for the outdoors, the trip to these islands may be the most rewarding Sleeping Bear experience of all.

Both are reached from Leland on Manitou Island Transit (231-256-9061), and each offers a different perspective.

South Manitou still has evidence of its years of human

habitation. There is an old schoolhouse, abandoned farms, a lighthouse (which was operated until 1958) and a cemetery. But life on the island was too difficult and its inhabitants eventually moved to the mainland.

The transit company offers motorized tours to several sites, both human and natural, during the summer months. The trips last for two hours and can be scheduled on the boat.

There are also several hiking trails. The most popular is a 6.9 mile loop to the southwestern tip of the island for a look at the giant cedars, the dunes and the clearly visible wreck of the *Francisco Morazan,* which went down in 1960.

The entire 15,000 acres of North Manitou is kept as a wilderness. There are no motor vehicles, designated campgrounds or services of any kind and all camping equipment must be carried in by backpack.

Reservations are strongly recommended for all trips to the islands. Scheduled departure time to South Manitou, June through August, is 10 a.m., daily, with check-in 45 minutes in advance. The crossing takes 90 minutes and the return trip leaves at 4:30 p.m. In May and early September, there are no trips on Tuesday and Thursday; weekends only, late September through October.

North Manitou departure times are the same in July and August. The crossing takes one hour and the boat stays just long enough to load and unload passengers. In early June, there are trips only on Wednesday and weekends, and in late June, there are no trips on Tuesday and Thursday. Call in advance for schedules in May and after September 1.

Information on fares and reservations is available at (231) 256-9061.

LEELANAU CONSERVANCY

Since its organization in 1988 this group has managed to preserve 3,500 acres of land and 8.5 miles of shoreline. Its 13 natural areas, some of which are closed to all outside intrusion and others open only for guided hikes, contain some of the most rewarding walking trails in the Leelanau. Here is a sampling of some of the best.

Houdek Dunes. 5 miles north of Leland, one mile past County Road 626. There are two trail loops of 1.5 and .75 miles. They are rated moderate in difficulty, with some sandy stretches and stairs to reach the crest of the dunes. Its most outstanding feature is the stand of white birches, some of the tallest and oldest in northern Michigan. There are also quaking aspen and "blow-out" dunes, where the sand has drifted around a large stand of green growth. The area is named for the family who farmed it in the late 19th Century. Portions of their farm can also be seen on this hike.

Boat on Kehl Lake

Kehl Lake. North from Northport on M-201. Left on Snyder Road, right on Sugarbush Road and then straight on Kehl Road. There are two loops with a total of 2 miles in trails. About three-quarters of the lakeshore lie within the area and there is a wealth of avian life; herons, kingfishers and loons. It is still called Leg Lake on some maps, a translation from the Ojibwa, who thought its outline resembled a deerskin legging. Some of the white pines in the forested area are thought to be more than 200 years old. There is also a viewing platform over the wetlands.

Chippewa Run. North from Empire on LaCore Street, then right on Fisher. There are no designated trails here but the Conservancy invites exploration by following deer trails or "find your own gaps in the grasses." This is a place for watching birds and marveling at the colorful diversity of wildflowers.

Much of the property was once cherry orchard and it was saved from development for housing by the Conservancy in 2000.

Whaleback. Just south of Leland, off M-22. The trail to the top of the dune is 1.5 miles and it is steep. This is one of the largest undeveloped stretches of the Lake Michigan shoreline in the Leelanau. You'll occasionally spot bald eagles from the viewing platform here and the trail leads past towering hemlock and hardwood forests.

Finton. North from Northport on M-201 and County Road 640 to Paradesia Road. A 35-acre patch of land amid a spectacular forest of hardwoods and cedars, near the northern tip of the peninsula.

You can obtain a schedule of guided walks from the Conservancy at (231) 256-9665.

Leelanau State Park

This is one of the jewels of Michigan's park system. At the very tip of the Leelanau Peninsula, the park's beaches are wrapped around **Cathead Bay**, a great source for Petoskey stones. There are 8.5 miles of hiking trails throughout the 1,350-acre park, and they lead to all the natural points of interest.

The grand attraction is the **Grand Traverse Lighthouse** (231-386-7195), built in 1852 to guard the entrance to Grand Traverse Bay. The keeper's home has been restored with many original furnishing and lighthouse instruments that make you feel as though you are in a working lighthouse. You also can climb to the top of the beacon tower, where the views are magnificent. On clear days you can see the following islands—**South Manitou, North Manitou,**

South Fox, North Fox and even **Beaver Island.** You can also see **Charlevoix.** The lighthouse is open daily, 10 a.m. to 7 p.m., June to Labor Day; noon to 4 p.m., May and Labor Day through October; weekends only, noon to 4 p.m., in November. Free with the admission fee to the park. When the museum is open, there is always a lighthouse keeper there to answer any questions, and they do give tours for youth and large groups, which encompass the grounds, the new lighthouse and the site of the old lighthouse.

The park can be reached by following M-201 and County Roads 640 and 629 north from Northport.

Leelanau Trail

This is an extension of the **TART Trail** that runs all the way across Traverse City. The final link between the two trails was completed in November, 2004, making it possible to walk from the eastern edge of Traverse City all the way to Suttons Bay.

The **Leelanau Trail** segment follows a former railroad right-of-way for 15 miles; past orchards and fields along a route that parallels M-22. It is level and paved for the entire distance, making it an easy excursion for novice hikers and bicyclists.

Bike Trips and Scenic Drives

Two of the most popular bike rides in the area circle the sections of Glen Lake. A narrow strip of land divides the lake. The part closest to Lake Michigan is called Little Glen Lake; the other and larger portion is known locally as (of course) Big Glen Lake.

The Little Glen Lake loop is rated more moderate in difficulty. It follows M-109 around the western shore, then east on County Road 616. Turn north across the narrows on M-22, then west along the lake's northern shore on Day Forest Road, which returns to M-109.

Inspiration Point

The Big Glen Lake loop ascends to two of the most famous viewpoints in the Leelanau. This ride starts at the lake narrows, heads east on County Road 616, and climbs to **Inspiration Point.** National Geographic Magazine once called Glen one of the five most beautiful lakes in the world. Part of the reason is this vista, across the water to the surrounding hills with Lake Michigan visible on the horizon.

Continue east on County Road 675, taking a breather at the **Old Settlers Picnic Grounds,** near Burdickville. The road then bends around the eastern shore of the lake. Watch for Cheney Road to the east and then take a north on Miller Hill Road.

This is a fairly strenuous workout, recommended only for more experienced cyclists. (Others can simply follow 675 back to its junction with M-22 at Glen Arbor.) Those who make the trek, though, will be rewarded with a spectacular view across the wooded hillsides and the lake from Miller Hill Lookout. Complete the trip by continuing on to Hyland Road, then left back to M-22 and Glen Arbor.

Another great ride destination is **Port Oneida Historic Farm District.** Technically not a ghost town, but close to it with abandoned farmsteads, a school and an old cemetery. Just north of Glen Arbor, off M-22. The place was settled

in 1852, and within 15 years it had a population of 87.
Most of them came from the Hanover region of Germany,
but they named the place after the first steamship to stop at
their new dock.

The short growing season defeated their best efforts to
make a living from this sandy soil and by the 1920s the
place was emptied out. The site is now part of Sleeping
Bear National Lakeshore and is treasured by photographers
for its wealth of old, abandoned barns. There are several
along Port Oneida Road, but the best known is the **Miller
Barn,** west on Miller Road, near the water. The National Park
Service warns that many of these barns are not structurally
stable and strongly advises against entering any of them.

All three of these rides are also perfectly suitable as
motorized scenic drives. But the top scenic ride in the area
is simply following M-22 all the way around the peninsula.
It is especially beautiful on the Grand Traverse Bay side, but
it is frequently in sight of the water and leads to almost
every major point of interest.

Rentals

The best source for bike and cross-country ski rentals in
the Leelanau is **Geo Bikes** (231-256-9696). They have a good
assortment of rental equipment and also do repairs. Location
is 102 S. Grand, Leland, just east of Main Street (M-22).

OTHER THINGS TO SEE

Leelanau Historical Museum. 231 East Cedar Street,
Leland. Open 10 a.m. to 4 p.m., Tuesday through Saturday;
Sunday, 1 p.m. to 4 p.m., June through Labor Day. Other
months, 10 a.m. to 4 p.m, Friday and Saturday.
(231) 256-7475.

This riverside museum has a very nice collection of

material from the Leelanau and its nearby islands, including artifacts belonging to early settlers, Native American crafts and displays on the area's maritime legacy. There is also a special room, conservation grade, on black ash baskets and quill work on birch bark—primarily from local Odawa artists. There is a museum store a few blocks away, on River Street, east of Main Street, with works by local artists and books on local history. It is open the same hours as the museum, but only during the summer months. One should note that this museum is always changing its exhibits, so if you have been before, it is always worth a trip back.

Empire Area Historical Museum. 11544 LaCore Street, Empire. Memorial Day through July 1 and Labor Day until early October, weekends 1 p.m. to 4 p.m., July 1 through Labor Day, open six days a week, 1 p.m. to 4 p.m., closed Wednesday. 231-326-5519.

Featuring a turn-of-the-century saloon, parlor, kitchen, blacksmith shop, 1911 vintage hose house (fire station) and complete one-room school preserved from the town's heyday as a Lake Michigan port.

WINERIES

In recent years, the 13 wineries of the Leelanau have become a star attraction. They are concentrated in the eastern part of the county with the biggest cluster near Suttons Bay. Each of them has a tasting room and many also host special events during the year. The wineries are listed in a south-to-north direction.

NOTE: All Sunday openings are at noon because of State liquor laws.

Harvest time happens in the Fall

Bel Lago. 6530 S. Lake Shore Drive, Cedar. (231) 228-4800. Daily, 11 a.m. to 6 p.m., May through October; November-December, noon to 5 p.m., rest of year, weekends only, noon to 5 p.m.

The name means "Beautiful Lake" and the vineyards spectacularly do indeed overlook South Lake Leelanau, on County Road 643, just south of Kabot Road. A bit off the beaten path, it might be for the more adventurous or for those willing to go further for a good wine. This is a 37-acre, family-owned winery, opened in 1987. Its Chardonnays have won awards in state-wide competitions.

Shady Lane Cellars. 9580 Shady Lane, Suttons Bay. (231) 947-8865. Daily, May-October, 11 a.m. to 6 p.m.; rest of year, weekends only.

The winery produces medal class methode champenoise sparking wines and a fine Chardonnay blanc de blanc. It also has the distinction of placing its tasting room in a century old cobblestone chicken coop. It's south of Suttons Bay and west from M-22 on Shady Lane.

Chateau de Leelanau. 5028 S.W. Bayshore Drive, Suttons Bay. (231) 271-8888. Daily, 11 a.m. to 6 p.m., June-December. Rest of year, closed Monday.

The "Andante" sparkling Riesling won medals at the 2003 Michigan State Fair and this winery, in operation since 1990, has been honored for its white varietals. The tasting room is in the silo of the one time farm, and it also houses a large gift shop. Just off M-22.

Willow Vineyard. 10702 E. Hilltop Road, Suttons Bay. (231) 271-4810. Wednesday-Sunday, May-October, noon-6 p.m.; weekends only, November-December.

A tiny operation with big views. Perched atop a hill overlooking the West Arm of Grand Traverse Bay—there are at least 10 miles of water view. Its specialty is Burgundy style wines, which you can only purchase from the winery.

Ciccone Vineyard. 10343 E. Hilltop Road, Suttons Bay. (231) 271-5551. Daily, noon-6 p.m., May-October; Thursday-Sunday, April and November. Saturday only, rest of year.

Opened since 1995 in a spectacular hilltop setting, this is another highly personalized boutique winery. Noted for its Chardonnays and the owner's superstar daughter, who isn't used for publicity, but easily could be.

L. Mawby. 4519 S. Elm Valley Road, Suttons Bay. (231) 271-3522. Daily, noon-6p.m., June-August. Thursday to Sunday, May and September-October; Saturday only, rest of year.

The *Detroit Free Press* called Larry Mawby, "the best of a new breed of Michigan winemakers." He lives up to this reputation by producing French-style sparkling wines of the highest quality. If you took this vineyard and put it in Champagne, France, you would call these wines champagne. The annual production is small, around 4,000 cases. Its tasting room is rustic and quaint, and open all year. Sparkling wines, traditional methods, handcrafted vintages. At the western end of the Hilltop Road row of wineries. Mawby himself is commonly on site and makes for a great conversation.

Black Star Farms. 10844 E. Revold Road, Suttons Bay. (231) 271-4884. Daily, 11 a.m. to 6 p.m., May-October; Closing at 5 p.m., rest of year.

This is a full scale agricultural operation, with a small inn, dairy barns, walking trails, cheese-making and some lovely hillside vineyards. Try the Pinot Gris and Pinot Noir. Between M-22 and County Road 633, south of Suttons Bay. As said before, this is as close to Napa Valley as you will find in Leelanau.

Bernie Rink examining a cluster of grapes at Boskydel Vineyards

Boskydel Vineyards. 7501 E. Otto Road, Lake Leelanau (231) 256-7272. Daily 1 p.m. to 6 p.m.

This was the first wine-making operation in the Leelanau. It was established in 1975 by Bernie Rink, a library director who read a book on vineyard cultivation and decided it could be done in this area. He tore up a baseball field on property he owned overlooking Lake Leelanau and started his plantings. Boskydel is still operated by Rink and many of the other wineries in the Leelanau were started up by its former employees. Its wide assortments of whites and fruit wines are always good.

Chateau Fontaine. 2290 S. French Road, Lake Leelanau. (231) 256-0000. Wednesday to Sunday, June-October, noon to 5 p.m.; weekends only, May and

November-December; rest of year, Saturday only.

Its address is a tribute to the French farmers who first settled this area, and the winery is named in tribute to them. The one-time potato farm was perfect for a vineyard because of its south-facing slopes, but its trademark also includes its west-facing sunsets. Known for Chardonnays and Gewurtztraminers. On County Road 645, north of County Road 620.

Good Harbor Vineyards. 34 S. Manitou Trail (M-22), Lake Leelanau. (231) 256-7165. Daily, late May-October. Saturday only, rest of year. Its Pinot Grigio has won awards in international competitions, and this family operation also turns out an excellent cherry wine.

Raftshol Vineyards. 1865 N. West Bay Drive (M-22), Suttons Bay. (231) 271-5650. Daily, noon-5p.m.

Another small operation, known for its Bordeaux wines, grown in defiance of the accepted wisdom that they could not thrive in this climate.

Gills Pier Winery. 5620 N. Manitou Trail (M-22), Northport. (231) 256-7003. Hours vary, call ahead.

Open only since 2000, the newest Leelanau winery already has won medals for its Riesling at State Fair competitions.

Leelanau Wine Cellars. 12683 E. Tatch Road (County Road 626), Omena. (231) 386-5201. Daily, 10 a.m. to 6 p.m., June-October. Rest of year, call for hours.

One of the oldest wineries in the area, it has been turning out excellent Chardonnays since 1975. Its late harvest Riesling is also highly regarded. Picnic grounds on the site.

FARM MARKETS

Think of the Leelanau as a vast garden, and in the late summer and early fall it is bursting with the bounty of the land. Farm markets are found throughout the peninsula, with the most intense concentration in its eastern half. Here is a sampling:

Westover Market, just west of Maple City, on County Road 616. (231) 228-5514. The most extensive U-pick operation for blueberries and raspberries. Open from 9 a.m. to 6 p.m., through October. There is also a stand with jams, maple syrup and veggies.

Alpers Berry Farm, west of M-22 at 1785 N. Setterbo Road, north of Suttons Bay. (231) 271-6656. Lots of raspberries with U-pick from midJuly to mid-August.

Bardenhagen Farms, north of Lake Leelanau on County Road 641, then east on Pertner Road. (231) 271-3199. Great assortment of peaches, nectarines and apricots. This is one of the major suppliers to area restaurants and stores. Call for hours.

Christmas Cove Farm, north from Northport on Kilcherman Road. (231) 386-5637. Its windmill is a local landmark. The market is open from mid-September to mid-November and its specialty is antique apple varieties, the kind you don't see at the supermarket. It also makes up gift boxes.

Covered Wagon Market, on M-204 between Suttons Bay and Lake Leelanau. (231) 271-6658. Great for summer vegetables, pumpkins, strawberries, both sweet and tart cherries and outstanding home-made baked fruit pies.

H&H Farm, east of Empire and south of M-72 on County 675 and Beeman Road. (231) 326-5150.

Watermelons, peppers, squash and older varieties of tomatoes.

Lanham Farm, south of Maple City on Newman Road then west on Kasson Center Road. (231) 228-5885. Terrific farm stand with honey, walnuts, peaches, pears and summer produce.

Swallow's Nest Farm, 9 miles north of Glen Arbor on M-22. (231) 228-4088. A fine selection of herbs, including good ones for cooking---thyme, cilantro, sage, dill.

TLC Tomatoes, north of Suttons Bay on M-22, then west on Setterbo Road. (231) 271-4754. The name says it all; hydroponic tomatoes in many varieties, along with cucumbers and lettuce. This is another restaurant supplier.

OTHER SHOPPING

Baa Baa ZuZu. The name sounds like the punch line to one of Johnny Carson's old Carnac the Magnificent routines. ("Question: Where do you put a sheep that's seeing double?") It specializes in boiled and reclaimed woolen clothes and every piece is a one-of-a-kind design. In Lake Leelanau, at 1006 Sawmill Road. (231) 256-7176.

Rimwalk Studio. The gallery sells the work of pastel artist Mary Fuscaldo, whose work you can see on the covers of the American Spoon catalogs. It's north of Cedar on County 645, then east on Hohnke Road and south, at 4249 S. Whitehill Drive. (231) 256-2237.

Pleva's Meats. This is the place that pioneered the use of cherry products with beef for a leaner sort of burger, Plevalean. It also has both cherry and meat products that remain separate. It's in Cedar on Kasson Street. (231) 228-5000).

Tamarack Craftsmen Gallery. Housed in a former barn and dance hall in Omena, it exhibits the works of more than 100 regional artists. Owner Sally Viskochil has used the gallery as the base for several cultural programs since opening it in 1970. (231) 386-5529.

Tamarack Craftsmen Gallery

GOLF

Dunes Golf Club. M-72, east of Empire. (231) 326-5390.

It bills itself as a "casual friendly course" and that pretty much tells the story. A good experience for beginners and some challenging holes on the back nine along tight, tree-lined fairways. The front nine opened in 1982, and the rest of the course followed nine years later. $37 with cart for 18 holes.

King's Challenge. South from M-22, on Lime Lake Road, between Glen Arbor and Leland. (888) 228-0121.

Arnold Palmer designed the course, which opened in 1998. It takes full advantage of the rolling terrain and forests, making it one of the most scenic courses in northern Michigan. Its dramatic 570-yard 5th hole plays across a valley and then comes up to a green guarded by two bunkers and a pond. Package deals can be made through the Homestead Resort. Rates for July and August run from $65 to $75.

Sleeping Bear Golf Club. This is the companion course to King's Challenge, one mile east at 4512 S. Townline Road. (888) 228-0121.

This was the first public course in the Leelanau, dating from the 1970s, and it is still among the friendliest. A few monster holes, such as the 618-yard 17th, and some narrow fairways. But still the easier of the two. Peak season rates are $38 to $43.

The Leelanau Club at Bahle Farms. Otto Road, west of County 633, south of Suttons Bay. (231) 271-2020.

Set among cherry orchards on property owned by the family that has run the Leelanau's oldest department store. This course is a unique experience when the trees come into blossom in early summer as two of the holes actually play through the orchards. Course architect Gary Pulsipher took full advantage of the rolling terrain. Peak season rates range from $59 to $69.

BEACHES

Being a peninsula, you might anticipate that there would be plenty of places to take a swim on the Leelanau. You will not be disappointed. On both the Lake Michigan and Grand Traverse Bay sides there are several outstanding beaches, and more on the interior lakes, Glen and Leelanau.

Lake Michigan

Empire Village Park. Niagara Street, Empire. In addition to a broad sandy beach it also has views up the line of dunes all the way to Sleeping Bear. Restrooms, picnic facilities.

Glen Haven Beach. Off M-209. Just outside the National Lakeshore in this historic village. It is usually quiet, being in a ghost town and all, but there are few facilities there.

On of the many beaches on Lake Michigan

Glen Arbor Municipal Beach. Foot of Lake Street, west from M-22 in the town of Glen Arbor. There are restrooms, picnic grounds and a playground.

Good Harbor Bay. Part of Sleeping Bear Dunes Lakeshore. At the end of Coleman Road (County 669) and at the start of the Good Harbor Bay hiking trail.

Good Harbor Beach. On a side road off M-22, south of Leland. Another lightly populated stretch of sand with minimal facilities.

Leland Municipal Beach. West from M-22 (Main Street). A pleasant city park with views of the marina and Fishtown, restrooms, picnic area.

Peterson Park. North from Northport on M-201, then west on Peterson Park Road. The beach is rocky, but this is prime Petoskey stone territory. Few facilities.

Leelanau State Park. Tip of the peninsula, at the end of County Road 629. At Lighthouse Point. State Park fees. Hiking trails and magnificent views across the bay. Very rocky.

Gills Pier. Midway between Leland and Northport. Turn west off of M-22 at the Happy Hour Restaurant and go down Gills Pier Road.

Nedow's Bay. On North Lake Leelanau. Take Pearl Street east from M-22 five blocks. Dock and sandy bottom with boat launch.

Grand Traverse Bay

Northport Beach. East of M-201, on Nagonaba Street. On a sheltered bay, the beach is part of a municipal park that also includes a marina and playground. There are restrooms nearby.

Suttons Bay Municipal Beach. East of M-22 and north of the marina. An exceptionally pleasant park, with nice views across to Stony Point. Playground and picnic grounds.

Elmwood Township Beach. M-22, just north of M-72, Greilickville. Right on the outskirts of Traverse City. Sand beach, restrooms, picnic grounds.

Inland Lakes

Glen Lake Beach. On M-109. Great views of the Dune Climb area right across the road. Restrooms, picnic grounds.

Old Settlers Park. On County Road 675, near Burdickville Road, a tranquil little park on the eastern edge of Big Glen Lake. Restrooms, playground, picnicking.

Centerville Township Park. South from the town of Lake Leelanau, on the west side of the lake, on County Road 643, near Hohnke Road. On South Lake Leelanau. Restrooms, picnic grounds, playground.

North Bar Lake. Just north of Empire, turn left off of M-22 and follow the signs. It is formed from a small inlet off of Lake Michigan. This small and warm lake is a beautiful spot.

FISHING

A charter boat entering Leland's Fishtown

Charters

Fishtown Charter Services. Leland. (231) 256-9639. Full and half-day charters aboard the 27-foot Tiara, berthed right at the Fishtown docks. Lake trout, brown trout, steelhead and salmon are caught on the big lake.

Whitecap Charters. Leland. (231) 256-7457. Capt. Jack Duff has fished Lake Michigan since 1966. Five and nine hour charters aboard the 26-foot *Whitecap*. Trips to the Manitou islands.

Showtime Charter Fishing. Cedar. (800) 817-5807. Specializing in trips upon the West Arm of Grand Traverse Bay on a 31-foot Tiara.

Crandell Charters. Suttons Bay. (231) 271-3643. Aboard a 28-foot Bertram into Grand Traverse Bay.

Fast Break. Northport. (231) 386-5777. Positioned for trips into the big lake or the bay aboard a 27-foot Chris Craft.

BOAT RENTALS

The two best sources are both located in Traverse City, but they will deliver to the Leelanau. They are **Native Wave Watersports** at (231) 938-3460 and **Sunset Rentals** at (231) 932-1800.

Kayak Leelanau is an excellent place for both the novice and experienced in this sport. It provides lessons, leads guided tours on nearby streams and into Lake Michigan; also plans independent trips. It's in Leland's Fishtown. (231) 256-8855.

Sleeping Bear Surf and Kayak also rents the right gear and specializes in trips along the big dunes. It is located in Empire, at 10085 W. Front Street. (231) 326-9283.

The Crystal River is one of the State's top streams for kayaking and tubing. It runs from Glen Lake to Lake Michigan, with its mouth at the Homestead Resort.
Best bet for rentals and guided trips is **Crystal River Outfitters,** at 6249 W. Western Avenue, Glen Arbor. (231) 334-4420.
Trips can also be arranged through **Orvis Streamside,** located at the Homestead and downtown Traverse City. Orvis also runs fishing trips for steelhead and salmon along the Crystal. (231-933-9300).

On the Narrows Marina at Glen Lake (800-772-9267), has a full line of fishing boats, ranging from 12 to 16 feet. Two-and-four-person sailboats are available, and so are pontoon boats that will hold up to 14 passengers. There are also pedal boats, kayaks and 17-foot canoes. The marina rents out water skis, wet suits, wake boards and outboard motors. All boats must remain on Glen Lake.

Besides its scenic attractions, this is also a fine fishing lake. You can expect to find perch, bass, pike, lake trout and splake.

On the Narrows is located at the M-22 bridge, 8137 S. Glen Lake Road. (800) 772-9267.

On Lake Leelanau is Narrows Passage, with pontoons, kayaks, canoes and fishing boats for rent. It is located just north of M-204, at 102 St. Marys Street, Lake Leelanau. (231) 256-2547. Smallmouth bass is the primary game fish on this lake.

There are also good fishing opportunities on Grand Traverse Bay from the public piers at Northport and Suttons Bay.

WINTER SPORTS

Most of the hiking trails in the Sleeping Bear Dunes National Lakeshore may be used for cross-country skiing. There are also guided snowshoe tours in the winter and snowshoes are provided. It is an excellent way to see the park in the winter. There are also cross-country and snow-shoe trails at Leelanau State Park and on the Leelanau Trail. Consult the hiking chapter for location and details. The Sleeping Bear park ranger also leads snowshoe hikes in the winter—a superb and informative adventure.

The only downhill runs in the Leelanau are at the Homestead Resort. There are 15 runs, the longest with a

375-foot drop and 1,320-foot length, and three lifts. Snow-boarders are welcomed on the resort's two terrain parks.

Sugar Loaf, near Cedar, a longtime ski resort in the area, is closed as of this writing. Plans to reopen or convert the area to other recreational purposes are on hold.

Best bet for ski rentals, if you are not a guest at a resort, is **Geo Bikes,** at 102 S. Grand, Leland. (231) 256-9696.

RAINY DAYS

1. There's always a winery.
2. Take in a movie at the Bay Theatre, the only cinema in the area, on St. Joseph Street, Sutton Bay.
3. The maritime museum at Glen Haven and the National Lakeshore visitors center, in Empire.
4. Gallery hop in Suttons Bay and Northport.

The Bay Theatre in Suttons Bay

KIDS

Sand Dune climbing

1. What kid can resist the Dune Climb?
2. Visit Lighthouse Point.
3. Look for Petoskey stones on the beach at Leelanau State Park.
4. Rent a paddle boat at Glen Lake.
5. Do a float trip down the Crystal River.

CASINO

Leelanau Sands is located in the historic Native American community of Peshawbestown, between Omena and Suttons Bay on M-22. It is run by the Grand Traverse Band of Ojibwa and Odawa and has been operating since 1984.

The casino has 416 slots in its 30,581 square foot casino and the usual table games. It operates a restaurant on the premises and a 51-room motel nearby.

Hours are 10 a.m. to 2 a.m., Sunday-Thursday; 3 a.m. on weekends. (231) 271-4104.

ANNUAL EVENTS

February:

Empire Winterfest. Second weekend. (231) 326-5249.
The winters are long and snowy here and this jolly gathering helps break the icy chain. Curling, dancing, community bonfire, ski race and the inevitable polar dip.

April:

Along the Leelanau Peninsula Wine Trail: Spring Sip and Savor. Last weekend. (231) 938-1811.
New wines are released and the scenery is coming into bloom.

May:

Lake Leelanau Walleye Tournament. Second Saturday. (231) 271-9895.
A competition to snare some of the tastiest game fish in the North.

June:

Leland Food and Wine Festival. Second Saturday. (231) 271-9895. The area's wineries and restaurants show off their goodies.

July:

Leland Artists' Market. Second Saturday. (231) 256-2131. One of the top shows in the Leelanau, with exhibits in the Old Art Building.

Glen Arbor Village Fair. Second weekend. (231) 334-3238. Sponsored by the Glen Lake Women's

Club, this is a venerable fest that features sidewalk sales, art displays, bake sales.

Cedar Polka Fest. First full weekend. (231) 271-9895. The town dances to the beat of its Polish heritage. There is a parade, too. An annual get-together since 1982.

Suttons Bay Jazz Festival. Fourth Saturday. (231) 271-4444. A celebration of classic jazz, New Orleans and big band style.

August:

Port Oneida Fair. First full weekend. (231) 326-5134. Rural culture in all its diversity in this historic farm district within the Sleeping Bear Lakeshore. Crafts demonstrations, food, barn tours.

Peshawbestown Pow-Wow. Third weekend. (231) 271-4104. One of the most important Native American gatherings in Michigan, with traditional music and dances, artwork, crafts.

Red, White and Blues Wine and Food Festival. Second Saturday, Northport. (231) 271-5077.
Sponsored by the Vintners Association, with good food and wine and great music.

September:

Leelanau Harvest Tour. Third Saturday. (231) 941-2453. This annual early autumn bike tour of the peninsula is put on by the Cherry Capital Cycling Club. Participants can take a variety of routes, run from 7 to 60 miles. Call for starting point and enrollment information.

HOSPITALS AND URGENT CARE

Leelanau Urgent Care.
6701 M-204, Lake Leelanau.
Just west of Lake Leelanau on M-204
(Duck Lake Road).
(231) 256-2273.

Sutton's Bay Urgent Care.
508 St. Joseph (M-22), Suttons Bay.
One block south of M-204 on M-22.
Open Friday, Saturday, and Sunday.
(231) 271-6511.